W9-CLV-408

Popular Rock Superstars of Yesterday and Today
POP ROCK

AC/DC	Elton John
Aerosmith	The Grateful Dead
The Allman Brothers Band	Led Zeppelin
The Beatles	Lynyrd Skynyrd
Billy Joel	Pink Floyd
Bob Marley and the Wailers	The Rolling Stones
Bruce Springsteen	U2
The Doors	The Who

Bob Marley
and the Wailers

Rosa Waters

Mason Crest Publishers

Bob Marley and the Wailers

FRONTIS   Bob Marley gave voice to an island nation and a new form of music—reggae.

Produced by 21st Century Publishing and Communications, Inc.

Editorial by Harding House Publishing Services, Inc.

MASON CREST PUBLISHERS INC.
370 Reed Road
Broomall, Pennsylvania 19008
(866) MCP-BOOK (toll free)
www.masoncrest.com

Printed in the United States.

First Printing

9 8 7 6 5 4 3 2 1

Library of Congress Cataloging-in-Publication Data

Waters, Rosa, 1957–
    Bob Marley and the Wailers / Rosa Waters.
       p. cm. — (Popular rock superstars of yesterday and today)
    Includes bibliographical references (p.   ) and index.
    Hardback edition: ISBN-13: 978-1-4222-0192-3
    Paperback edition: ISBN-13: 978-1-4222-0317-0
  1. Marley, Bob—Juvenile literature. 2. Singers—Jamaica—Biography—Juvenile literature. 3. Wailers (Reggae group)—Juvenile literature. 4. Reggae musicians—Jamaica—Biography—Juvenile literature. I. Title.
ML3930.M315W38 2008
782.421646092—dc22
[B]   2007012148

Publisher's notes:
- All quotations in this book come from original sources, and contain the spelling and grammatical inconsistencies of the original text.

- The Web sites mentioned in this book were active at the time of publication. The publisher is not responsible for Web sites that have changed their addresses or discontinued operation since the date of publication. The publisher will review and update the Web site addresses each time the book is reprinted.

CONTENTS

ROCK 'N' ROLL TIMELINE

1951
"Rocket 88," considered by many to be the first rock single, is released by Ike Turner.

1952
DJ Alan Freed coins and popularizes the term "Rock and Roll," proclaimes himself the "Father of Rock and Roll," and declares, "Rock and Roll is a river of music that has absorbed many streams: rhythm and blues, jazz, rag time, cowboy songs, country songs, folk songs. All have contributed to the Big Beat."

1955
"Rock Around the Clock" by Bill Haley & His Comets is released; it tops the U.S. charts and becomes wildly popular in Britain, Australia, and Germany.

1967
The Monterey Pop Festival in California kicks off open air rock concerts.

1965
The psychedelic rock band, the Grateful Dead, is formed in San Francisco.

1969
The Woodstock Music and Arts Festival attracts a huge crowd to rural upstate New York.

1969
Tommy, the first rock opera, is released by British rock band The Who.

1970
The Beatles break up.

1971
Jim Morrison, lead singer of The Doors, dies in Paris.

1971
Duane Allman, lead guitarist of the Allman Brothers Band, dies.

1950s

1960s

1970s

1957
Bill Haley tours Europe.

1957
Jerry Lee Lewis and Buddy Holly become the first rock musicians to tour Australia.

1954
Elvis Presley releases the extremely popular single "That's All Right (Mama)."

1961
The first Grammy for Best Rock 'n' Roll Recording is awarded to Chubby Checker for *Let's Twist Again*.

1964
The Beatles make their first visit to America, setting off the British Invasion.

1969
A rock concert held at Altamont Speedway in California is marred by violence.

1969
The Rolling Stones tour America as "The Greatest Rock and Roll Band in the World."

1973
Rolling Stone magazine names Annie Leibovitz chief photographer and "rock 'n' roll photographer;" she follows and photographs rockers Mick Jagger, John Lennon, and others.

1974
Sheer Heart Attack by the British rock band Queen becomes an international success.

1974
"Sweet Home Alabama" by Southern rock band Lynyrd Skynyrd is released and becomes an American anthem.

1987
Billy Joel becomes the first American rock star to perform in the Soviet Union since the construction of the Berlin Wall.

2005
Led Zeppelin is ranked #1 on VH1's list of the 100 Greatest Artists of Hard Rock.

1985
Rock stars perform at Live Aid, a benefit concert to raise money to fight Ethiopian famine.

2005
Many rock groups participate in Live 8, a series of concerts to raise awareness of extreme poverty in Africa.

2003
Led Zeppelin's "Stairway to Heaven" is inducted into the Grammy Hall of Fame.

1980
John Lennon of the Beatles is murdered in New York City.

2000s
Aerosmith's album sales reach 140 million worldwide and the group becomes the bestselling American hard rock band of all time.

2007
Billy Joel become the first person to sing the National Anthem before two Super Bowls.

1975
Tommy, the movie, is released.

1975
Time magazine features Bruce Springsteen on its cover as "Rock's New Sensation."

1995
The Rock and Roll Hall of Fame and Museum opens in Cleveland, Ohio.

1970s   1980s   1990s   2000s

1979
Pink Floyd's *The Wall* is released.

1991
Freddie Mercury, lead vocalist of the British rock group Queen, dies of AIDS.

2004
Elton John receives a Kennedy Center Honor.

1979
The first Grammy for Best Rock Vocal Performance by a Duo or Group is awarded to The Eagles.

2004
Rolling Stone Magazine ranks The Beatles #1 of the 100 Greatest Artists of All Time, and Bob Dylan #2.

1986
The Rolling Stones receive a Grammy Lifetime Achievement Award.

1981
MTV goes on the air.

2006
U2 wins five more Grammys, for a total of 22—the most of any rock artist or group.

1986
The first Rock and Roll Hall of Fame induction ceremony is held; Chuck Berry, Little Richard, Ray Charles, Elvis Presley, and James Brown, are among the first inductees.

1981
For Those About to Rock We Salute You by Australian rock band AC/DC becomes the first hard rock album to reach #1 in the U.S.

2006
Bob Dylan, at age 65, releases *Modern Times* which immediately rises to #1 in the U.S.

Though Bob Marley died in 1985, his influence, and that of the Wailers, has endured. He introduced the world to a new music style—reggae—and even to a religion—Rastafarianism—that was unknown to most people. And the world hasn't forgotten Bob and his contributions, both in and out of music.

Gone but Not Forgotten

On February 6, 2001, a new star was added to the Hollywood Walk of Fame. Bob Marley of the reggae group the Wailers received the star in honor of his fifty-sixth birthday. Unfortunately, Bob could not be there to enjoy the honor; he had died in 1985. However, his friends, family, and fans celebrated on his behalf.

Barbara Barabino of Ragga Muffins Productions was the one who had made it all happen. She told the Associated Press:

> **"I had this dream over 10 years ago and basically wondered why Bob didn't have such a recognition. Nevertheless, I started the process, and this was my third application to nominate Brother Bob. I made the applications, circulated petitions, procured letters and finally it happened."**

Barbara added:

❝I salute Reggae music, all the artists in the industry, and the many fans who come out every year in celebration of Bob's birthday. As Bob's message lives on in us, we too advocate social unity and will 'emancipate ourselves from mental slavery,' one of the most significant and challenging statements left to us by Brother Bob. Bob's music has and will continue to touch the lives of millions around the globe.❞

Honor After Honor

Bob's star was not the only **posthumous** recognition he had received. The same month he received his star on the Walk of Fame, he was also awarded the Grammy Lifetime Achievement Award.

And seven years earlier, in 1994, Bob had been **inducted** into the Rock and Roll Hall of Fame. This meant he would take his place in the Hall's permanent museum in Cleveland, Ohio. That night at the Waldorf-Astoria in New York City, nearly thirteen years after his death, his family and friends were there to pay tribute. Other inductees included the Animals, the Band, Duane Eddy, the Grateful Dead, Elton John, John Lennon, Johnnie Otis, and Rod Stewart, all music legends in their own right—but none of them overshadowed Bob's legacy.

A Legacy of Justice

That night, rock historian Warren Zanes, the Hall's vice president of education, reminded the crowd that Bob's courageous voice as he spoke out against racism in Jamaica had set an example for others in his field.

❝Because of the post-colonial situation in Jamaica ... with a lot of poverty and racial strife, because that was so much in his music, he showed what music could look like when it was deeply engaged with social and political meaning.❞

Bob's heritage of justice and courage made it especially appropriate that he be inducted into the Hall by another prolific musician and

On February 5, 2001, Rita Marley and her children celebrated Bob's fifty-sixth birthday by unveiling his star on the famous Hollywood Walk of Fame. Now, visitors to Hollywood can pay their respects to the late reggae star as well as to many others who have made a contribution to the arts.

humanitarian—U2's lead singer Bono. Speaking before an audience that included Bob's widow, Rita, his sons Ziggy, Ky-mani, and Julian, his mother, Cedella Marley Booker, and various members of Bob's band, the Wailers, Bono said that Bob "didn't walk down the middle," but instead, he "raced to the edges, embracing all extremes and creating a oneness—his oneness of love."

In his speech, Bono also recalled a trip that he and his wife Ali took to Ethiopia, where "everywhere we went, we saw Bob Marley's face . . . royal, wise. . . . on every street corner, there he was, dressed to hustle God. . . . 'Let my people go,' an ancient plea. . . . Prayers catching fire in Mozambique, Nigeria, the Lebanon, Alabama, Detroit, New York, Notting Hill, Belfast. . . . Dr. King in dreads."

Zanes spoke out in recognition of the connection between Bob and Bono:

Rock fans are scheduled to have their own theme park as of 2008. When ground was broken for the Hard Rock Park in Myrtle Beach, South Carolina, on July 13, 2006, the shovelers were watched by a gigantic sand sculpture of four of the biggest names in rock history: Elvis Presley, Jimi Hendrix, John Lennon, and Bob Marley—"Mount Rockmore."

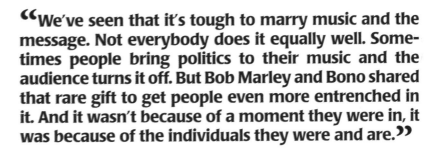

❝We've seen that it's tough to marry music and the message. Not everybody does it equally well. Sometimes people bring politics to their music and the audience turns it off. But Bob Marley and Bono shared that rare gift to get people even more entrenched in it. And it wasn't because of a moment they were in, it was because of the individuals they were and are.❞

Bob Would Have Been Happy

Bob's widow, Rita, was pleased with the evening's events. If Bob could have been there, she said, he would have nodded "his head in consent." She continued:

❝I remember when we were back in Trenchtown and we wondered if we would ever be able to get an award, a Grammy. We'd laugh and say we were crazy, we'd never get there. But we did.❞

The induction ceremony was an evening of brilliant star power. Some of the musicians in the house that night included Paul McCartney of the Beatles; John Lennon's widow Yoko and their son, Sean Lennon; Bruce Springsteen; Eric Clapton; Chuck Berry; Axl Rose; Etta James; Mariah Carey; and Bruce Hornsby. Stars of the acting world were there as well: Robert DeNiro, Martin Scorsese, Whoopi Goldberg, and Naomi Campbell.

Following Rock and Roll Hall tradition, the evening was capped off with an all-star jam session featuring the inductees' classic music. For Marley fans, the evening's high point was the rendition of Bob's hit song, "One Love," with Rita, Ziggy, Bono, and others trading verses.

Pure Rock

American music critic Timothy White, author of *Catch a Fire: The Life of Bob Marley*, wrote of Bob Marley: "His music was pure rock, in the sense that it was a public expression of a private truth."

Bob's private truth, however, was one shared by countless blacks whose ancestors had been brought to the Americas as slaves. His music gave voice to the justice they deserved.

Jamaican culture gave rise to the sounds that would be forever identified with Bob Marley and the Wailers. Race, politics, and religion were major influences on the lives of Bob and his Wailers. Drawing from his life experiences, those influences also made their way into the music that made Bob Marley and the Wailers famous.

2

Jamaica's Voice

Bob Marley and the Wailers were born on the island of Jamaica, a small land with deep roots in Africa. Slavery was a recent folk memory for the island's residents, and twentieth-century racial injustice continued to lay a heavy hand on Jamaica. It was this rich and troubled culture that gave birth to the music of Bob Marley.

Politics and Faith

At the start of the twentieth century, Marcus Garvey, a shrewd Jamaican preacher and businessman, **advocated** for the creation of a new black state in Africa, free from white domination. A few years later, in 1930, Ras Tafari Makonnen was crowned emperor of Ethiopia and took a new name, Haile Selassie. The emperor claimed to be the 225th ruler in a line that stretched back to Menelik, the son of Solomon and Sheba. Back in Jamaica, Marcus

Garvey's followers believed Haile Selassie was the black king whom Garvey had prophesied would deliver his people. This was the start of a new religion called Rastafari, a faith that would have a strong influence on Bob Marley and the Wailers.

Island Music

Robert Nesta Marley was born in 1945. His mother was an eighteen-year-old black girl named Cedella Booker who had married Captain Norval Marley, a fifty-year-old white **quartermaster** with the British West Indian Regiment. Norval Marley's family did not approve of his marriage, and Bob seldom saw his father as he was growing up in the island's northern countryside.

When Bob was in his teens, he and his mother moved to Kingston, where they settled in the slums of Trenchtown. As Bob grew older, his friends were other street youths. One friend in particular was Neville O'Riley Livingston, known as Bunny. The two young men were fascinated by the music they picked up from American radio stations, particularly a New Orleans station that broadcast the latest tunes by Ray Charles, Fats Domino, Curtis Mayfield, and Brook Benton. Bob and Bunny also paid close attention to the black vocal groups such as the Drifters.

During these years, Bob met up with the Rastas, a group of marijuana-smoking, Bible-quoting preachers. Bob, however, had only one ambition—music—and religion did not yet hold that much appeal for him. He quit school, took a job in a welding shop, and spent all his free time with Bunny, perfecting their vocal abilities.

They were helped by one of Trenchtown's famous residents, the singer Joe Higgs who held informal lessons for **aspiring** vocalists in the tenement yards. At one of those sessions, Bob and Bunny met Peter McIntosh, another young man with musical ambitions.

The Wailing Wailers

In 1962, Bob Marley auditioned for a local music **entrepreneur** named Leslie Kong. Impressed by the quality of Bob's voice, Kong cut some tracks of his songs; "Judge Not" became Marley's first record.

The following year, Bob, Bunny, and Peter formed the Wailing Wailers. The new group's **mentor** was a Rastafarian hand drummer named Alvin Patterson, who introduced the young men to Clement

Dodd, a record producer in Kingston. In the summer of 1963, Dodd auditioned the Wailing Wailers and then agreed to record the group.

Ska

Ska was a hot, new dance-floor music with a pronounced backbeat that sprang from both Jamaica's African heritage and the sounds of New Orleans that traveled to the island on radio waves. Sound systems on the streets of Kingston spread ska across the island. Clement "Sir Coxsone" Dodd was one of the city's finest sound-system men.

During the last weeks of 1963, the Wailing Wailers released their first single, "Simmer Down," a ska tune put out on the Coxsone label. By the following January, it was #1 on the Jamaican charts, a position

In 1963, Bob Marley, Neville O'Riley Livingston—Bunny, and Peter McIntosh—Peter Tosh—(left to right) became the Wailing Wailers. Influenced by music coming out of the United States as well as ska, the hottest sound on the island nation, the group had its first #1 hit in Jamaica in January 1964.

it held for the next two months. The group—Bob, Bunny, and Peter, together now with Junior Braithwaite and backup singers, Beverly Kelso and Cherry Smith—were the island's biggest news.

The Wailing Wailers began recording regularly for Coxsone Dodd's Studio One Company. The group's music was the voice of the slums' street rebels. The Wailing Wailers gave Jamaican music a new angry, urban sound.

America and Marriage

Despite the group's popularity, money was tight, and three of its members—Junior Braithwaite, Beverly Kelso, and Cherry Smith—quit. Meanwhile, Bob's mother, Cedella, had remarried and moved to Delaware in the United States; once she had saved enough money, she sent her son a plane ticket so he could join her.

But before Bob moved to America, he met a young girl named Rita Anderson. On February 10, 1966, they were married.

Bob's stay in America was a short one. He worked just enough to finance his real ambition: music. After eight months, he returned to Jamaica.

Bob Marley and Rastafarianism

When Bob came back to Kingston, he found that Rastafarianism had taken on new life. Bob was now increasingly drawn to these beliefs, and by 1967, his music reflected his new faith. His angry street songs disappeared, and in their place was a growing commitment to spiritual and social issues.

The Rastafarians' faith is famous for its belief that the Bible approves of smoking marijuana. Contrary to common thought, however, Rastafarians do not smoke marijuana recreationally. Instead, they refer to it as "wisdom weed," and they believe it aids meditation and spiritual awakening. They base their use of marijuana on these Bible verses:

> **"Thou shalt eat the herb of the field."** (Genesis 3:18)
>
> **"Eat every herb of the land."** (Exodus 10:12)
>
> **"Better is a dinner of herb where love is, than a stalled ox and hatred there with."** (Proverbs 15:17)
>
> **"He causeth the grass for the cattle, and herb for the service of man."** (Psalms 104:14)

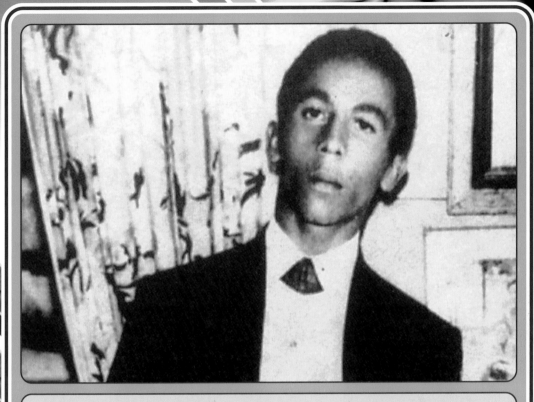

It wasn't all about music for Bob. He also found the time to meet and fall in love with Rita Anderson. In this photo, Bob is shown on his wedding day, February 10, 1966. Not long after the wedding, the young couple moved to the United States to join Bob's mother.

Dreadlocks are also associated with Rastafarianism. These matted locks of hair symbolize the Rasta roots; they call attention to the Rastas' African heritage because they are such a contrast to the straight, light-colored hair of white people.

However, according to author E. Cashmore, who has written several books on Rastafarianism, the most central **tenet** of Rastafarianism is the concept "I and I":

"a complex term that refers to the oneness of Jah (God) and every human. According to the faith, God is in all of us, and we are in fact one people. I and I is an

After a brief stay in the United States, Bob and Rita returned to Jamaica, where he was reintroduced to Rastafarianism. When the group re-formed as The Wailers, the influence of Rastafarianism on the music was clear. Anger was replaced by a commitment to social issues, and the song lyrics showed that evolution.

expression to totalize the concept of oneness, the oneness of two persons. So God is within all of us and we're one people in fact. I and I means that God is in all men. The bond of Ras Tafari is the bond of God, of man. But man itself needs a head and the head of man is His Imperial Majesty Haile Selassie I of Ethiopia.**"**

The Wailers Reborn

Inspired by Rastafarianism, Marley was ready to make music. He joined up again with Bunny and Peter to re-form the group, now known as the Wailers. Jamaican music, meanwhile, was changing. The bouncy ska beat had been replaced by a slower pace called rocksteady. These slower rhythms found their way into the Wailers' songs.

The Wailers' new commitment to Rastafarianism brought them into conflict with their old sponsor, Coxsone Dodd. Determined to control its destiny, the group formed its own record label, Wail 'N' Soul. Despite a few early successes, however, the Wailers' lack of business experience became fatal, and the label folded in late 1967. The group survived, however, initially as songwriters for a company associated with the American singer Johnny Nash, who eventually had an international smash hit with Marley's "Stir It Up."

Reggae

The Wailers' music started a new musical **genre**—reggae, a sound that's built on backbeats. According to one reggae musician, quoted on BobMarley.com, this new genre meant that:

> **"**You'd watch the bass player and the drummer. I could never get the American guys to play that way. You have to have a social experience to realize that this music is on the other beat. Once you get past the awkwardness of not knowing what the other beat is, you are seduced by the whole thing.**"**

Africa's rhythms were clearly heard in reggae. At last, Jamaica had found its voice. And Bob Marley and the Wailers were the ones who made the whole world listen.

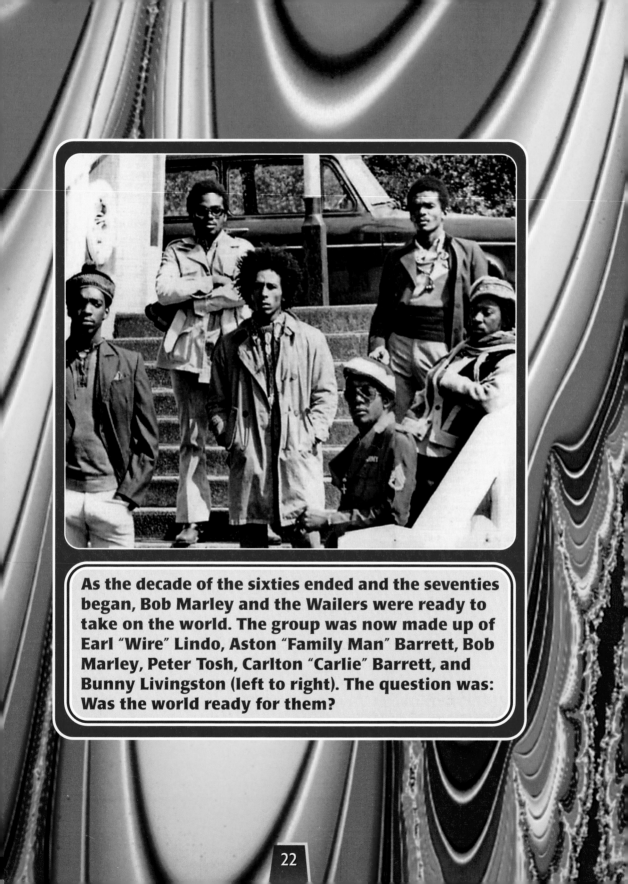

As the decade of the sixties ended and the seventies began, Bob Marley and the Wailers were ready to take on the world. The group was now made up of Earl "Wire" Lindo, Aston "Family Man" Barrett, Bob Marley, Peter Tosh, Carlton "Carlie" Barrett, and Bunny Livingston (left to right). The question was: Was the world ready for them?

3

The Wailers Become International

As the 1970s got going, Bob Marley and the Wailers were famous throughout the Caribbean. On the island nations scattered across the Caribbean Sea's warm blue waters, everyone was moving to the beat of Bob and his group. Internationally, however, they were still unknown. But that was about to change.

New Members

In 1970, Aston "Family Man" Barrett on the bass guitar and his brother Carlton on the drums joined the Wailers. The Barrett brothers were famous for being Jamaica's finest masters of rhythm, a status that remained theirs throughout the following decade.

In a 1999 interview with Duggy Bones, Family Man described his musical background:

> **I listen to some great music in my early years, a mixture of music was on Jamaican radio. By listening to the favorite players—Lloyd Brevett, Lloyd Spence, Jackie Jackson—and I grab off their style and then I'd improvise. In those days we always structure the music dem with more arrangements. I also love singing but I'm not really a singer professionally, so when I am playing I pretend that I am singing baritone. The bass so, I make a line, fill in the gaps to make the singer flow more, give the drummer that space to drop, feel it on the one drop. The drummer is the heartbeat and the drummer is the backbone.**

In the same interview, Family Man talked about the first time he heard Bob Marley and the Wailers:

> **The first time I hear that group do that music called Simmer Down we were on the western side of Kingston, on Olympic Way. . . . and my friend say, 'Come inside here and listen to this new group on the jukebox.' . . . Believe you me, no other music played 'til we were ready to leave that place, pure simmer down, simmer down, simmer down, until I feel like I was a part of the group at that time. I didn't play the music yet, but when I meditate on it deep down, I say, 'I like what these guys sound.' I listen for their future recordings.**

Not too long later, Family Man got a message that Bob needed him for a session. Family Man was amazed—but so was Bob when he met Family Man. Bob had never imagined he would be so young!

The Wailers in Britain

In the summer of 1971, Bob accepted an invitation from Johnny Nash to accompany him to Sweden where the American singer had taken a film-score commission. While in Europe, Bob secured a record contract with CBS, the same company that produced Nash's music. By the following spring, all the Wailers were in London to promote their CBS single, "Reggae on Broadway."

Instead they found themselves stranded in Britain with no money, no backing, and no plan. Desperate, Bob walked into the Basing Street Studios of Island Records and asked to see its founder, Chris Blackwell.

Island Records had been the major impetus behind the rise of Jamaican music in Britain. The company also produced white rock music, including such bands and artists as Traffic, Jethro Tull, King Crimson, Cat Stevens, Free, and Fairport Convention. When Bob contacted Blackwell in 1971, he was connecting with the hottest

In 1971, Bob Marley and the Wailers were stranded in Britain. But instead of wallowing in self-pity, Bob and the rest of the band took matters into their own hands. They contacted one of the biggest recording companies in the country, and before long, they had a new record contract, appearances on the BBC, and money to make an album.

independent record company in the world at that time. Blackwell already knew of the Wailers' Jamaican reputation, and now he offered them a deal. He advanced the Wailers £4000 to make an album and gave them access to recording facilities.

Breaking the Rules

Before this deal, reggae music had sold only on singles and cheap compilation albums. But the Wailers' first album, *Catch a Fire*, broke all the rules for reggae music. It was professionally packaged and heavily promoted. This album was the Wailers' first step on their long climb to international fame and recognition.

Years later, the reggae **dub** poet Linton Kwesi Johnson wrote about *Catch a Fire*:

> **"A whole new style of Jamaican music has come into being. It has a different character, a different sound . . . what I can only describe as International Reggae. It incorporates elements from popular music internationally: rock and soul, blues and funk. These elements facilitated a breakthrough on the international market."**

Catch a Fire was not an immediate hit, but the critics were impressed. The album received plenty of media attention. The strong dance rhythms combined with Bob's militant lyrics created a fresh new sound that stood out from mainstream rock.

Island Records decided the Wailers should go on tour, both in Britain and America. Once again, this was something no one expected a reggae band to do. But in April 1973, Bob and his band went on a club tour, starting out in London. These performances created the Wailers' reputation as a live group.

After three months, however, the band returned to Jamaica. Bunny didn't like life on the road, and he refused to play for the American tour. Joe Higgs, the Wailers' original singing teacher, took his place.

Finding Fame

The Wailers' American tour drew packed houses. It even included a weekend engagement with a young new rock star named Bruce

Springsteen. Seventeen concerts were scheduled with Sly & the Family Stone, then the number-one band in black American music.

Four shows into the tour, however, the Wailers were taken off the bill. They were *too* good; audiences liked them better then Sly & the

When the Wailers toured the United States, they found a very enthusiastic audience that grew with each performance. Concerts with Sly & the Family Stone were huge hits, especially for the Wailers. In fact, the Wailers were too popular and were fired after only four concerts of a seventeen-concert series.

Family Stone. The Wailers made their way alone to San Francisco. There they broadcast a live concert for the pioneering rock radio station, KSAN. Nearly twenty years later, in 1991, Island Records released the music from that concert on a **commemorative** album, *Talkin' Blues.*

In 1973, the Wailers released their second album with Island Records, *Burnin'*, which included new versions of some of the band's older songs—"Duppy Conqueror," "Small Axe," and "Put It On"— along with newer tracks such as "Get Up Stand Up" and "I Shot the Sheriff." This last song became a worldwide hit for Eric Clapton the following year, reaching #1 on the U.S. singles' chart.

Singing for Justice

Like many of Bob's songs, "I Shot the Sheriff" was more than just a catchy tune; it was an anthem for justice. No matter how much success came his way, Bob never forgot the world of poverty and prejudice where he had grown up. His mission was to give voice to the innocent who suffered at the hands of the powerful.

Bob was known for his **optimism**; his faith in God filled him with hope. But Bob expressed his darker side in the song "I Shot the Sheriff." In a 1970s interview, Bob said, "I was born with a price on my head." In other words, as a black man, he was automatically in trouble with the authorities.

The song also begins with the speaker already in trouble: "All around in my home town/They are trying to track me down." The song's narrator knows the system is stacked against him. Sheriff John Brown harassed him, forcing him at last to defend himself. And now he will be tried for double murder— not only the sheriff's death, for which he admits he is responsible, but for the deputy's death as well, an act for which he was not responsible.

"Ev'ry time I plant a seed," the song says, the sheriff responds, "Kill it before it grows." The seed in the song stands for the Rastafarians' ideas: their beliefs in justice, equality, and freedom, ideas that were considered dangerous by the white authorities—ideas that had to be squashed before they could grow and threaten the status quo.

Many artists use their songs to express opinions about conditions in the world. This has probably been done since the time of the very first song. Bob also used his music to express his dismay about the conditions he saw—and had lived in. He gave those without a voice a vehicle through which their plight could be heard.

In the song's final stanza, the narrator says,

> " Freedom came my way one day,
> And I started out of town.
> All of a sudden I saw Sheriff John Brown
> Aiming to shoot me down.
> So I shot, I shot, I shot him down. "

When Bob sang his hit "I Shot the Sheriff," he was singing about justice and freedom, basic ideas behind his religion, Rastafarianism. Everyone could enjoy the song at its surface level, but those who were ready to dive a little deeper received an education about some of the social problems of the day.

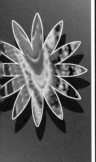

In other words, this was not a fight the speaker wanted. But if he were to survive, he was left with no choice. "Reflexes had the better of me," he says. According to *Rastafari: An Ancient Tradition*, reflexes are good things; they are God-given traits that are expressed when human beings are in their natural, original innocence. They are the expression of "I and I," humanity's union with God.

The song's speaker then says, "Every day the bucket a go a well/One day the bottom a go drop out." This is a Jamaica folk saying that means if something happens often enough, there are bound to be consequences. In this case, when injustice is repeated over and over, sooner or later violence will erupt. But who is really at fault here? The song's narrator who did in fact kill the sheriff—or the corrupt system that allowed the sheriff to abuse his power in the first place?

The Rastafarians viewed the government, the police, and the courts as "servants of Babylon"—the evil kingdom that, according to the Bible, forced God's children into submission. The Rastas identified with the Children of Israel; they found inspiration and comfort in the Bible's stories of freedom and righteousness. Claiming the Bible's authority, the Rastas stood up for their own dignity, their right to live on moral grounds in a system that would deny their existence. It is this voice that speaks through Bob's lyrics in "I Shot the Sheriff."

The Power of Music

Bob spoke out for justice and integrity in many of his other songs as well. In "Zimbabwe," he sang, "Brother you're right, you're right. . . . We gonna fight, fight for our rights." In "Get Up Stand Up," he sang, "And now you see the light/You stand up for your rights." His message was a timeless one, and people around the world identified with it. What's more, he had the white mainstream population humming along with his songs of revolution.

The year after the release of *Burnin'*, Bob spent much of his time working in the recording studio. These sessions eventually produced *Natty Dread*, an album that included songs such as "Talkin' Blues," "No Woman No Cry," "So Jah Seh," "Revolution," "Them Belly Full (But We Hungry)," and "Rebel Music (3 O'clock Roadblock)."

Bob's lyrics were both fierce and joyful. America loved the happy rhythm of his music—and they took notice of his cries for justice. Bob recognized the strength of his message. He said:

The music of Bob Marley and the Wailers didn't just touch the people of his native Jamaica. The problems the Wailers sang about—poverty, racism and prejudice, and violence— were issues faced by those living in countries all over the world. The Wailers' ability to touch the minds and hearts of so many made them a big hit worldwide.

> **"My music will go on forever. Maybe it's a fool say that, but when me know facts me can say facts. My music will go on forever."**

However, Bob was never arrogant. While he knew his music had power, he took no credit for it personally. Instead, he gave all credit to Jah (God):

> **"People want to listen to a message, word from Jah. This could be passed through me or anybody. I am not a leader. [I'm a] messenger. The words of the songs, not the person, is what attracts people."**

Changing the World

Bob was ambitious, but not in the same way most musicians were in the 1970s. Instead, his biggest ambitions were for humanity, rather than for himself. He said:

> **"Me only have one ambition, y'know. I only have one thing I really like to see happen. I like to see mankind live together—black, white, Chinese, every-one—that's all."**

Bob Marley and the Wailers were certainly changing the music world. But big changes were coming for the Wailers themselves. By the start of 1975, Bunny and Peter decided to quit the band permanently. They launched out on their own as Bunny Wailer and Peter Tosh. The band needed new members.

The mid-1970s brought a new version of the Wailers. But the group's membership wasn't the only thing that had changed. Reggae now had a significant part in mainstream music, and much of the credit goes to Bob Marley and the Wailers. Their music was more popular than ever, but it never lost its edge.

4

The New Wailers

By the summer of 1975, the band was on the road again. Bob's wife Rita, Marcia Griffiths, and Judy Mowatt formed a trio called the I-Threes that sang backup, replacing Bunny and Peter's harmonies. The "new" Wailers also included Carlton and Aston Barrett, Junior Marvin, Al Anderson, Tyrone Downie, Earl "Way" Lindo, and Alvin "Seeco" Patterson.

Superstars

Two of the tour's shows were at the Lyceum Ballroom in London, and these concerts are still remembered as some of the decade's brightest highlights. The shows were recorded, and the subsequent live album, together with the single "No Woman No Cry," both made the charts.

The mid-1970s brought the I-Threes into Bob Marley and the Wailers' fold. Bob's wife Rita, Marcia Griffiths, and Judy Mowatt made up the group that replaced Bunny and Peter, two of the original Wailers. The different sound didn't harm the popularity of the group. Rather, the group had some of its biggest hits with the I-Threes singing backup.

It was definite now: Bob Marley and the Wailers had managed to take reggae into the mainstream. By November, when the Wailers returned to Jamaica to play a benefit concert with Stevie Wonder, they were obviously their country's greatest superstars.

Rastaman Vibration, the album they produced the following year in 1976, cracked the American charts at #8. It included the songs "Crazy Baldhead," "Johnny Was," "Who the Cap Fit," and, perhaps most important, "War." The lyrics of this song were taken from a speech by Ethiopian emperor Haile Selassie, whom the Rastafarians claimed as God's representative on earth:

"Until the philosophy which hold one race superior and another inferior is finally and totally discredited

and abandoned; that until there are no longer first class and second class citizens of any nation; until the color of a man's skin is of no more significance than the color of his eyes; that until the basic human rights are equally guaranteed to all, without regard to race; that until that day, the dream of lasting peace, world citizenship, the rule of international morality will remain but a fleeting illusion to be pursued but never attained. And until the ignoble and unhappy regime that hold our brothers in Angola, in Mozambique, in South Africa, in sub-human bondage, have been toppled, utterly destroyed; until that day the African continent will not know peace. We Africans will fight we find it necessary. And we know we shall win, as we are confident in the victory of good over evil. **"**

Rastaman Vibration's international success cemented Bob's growing political importance in Jamaica, where his firm Rastafarian stance spoke clearly to the ghetto youth.

Violence

As a thank you to the people of Jamaica, Marley decided to give a free concert, called Smile Jamaica, at Kingston's National Heroes Park on December 5, 1976. Bob wanted to emphasize the need for peace in the slums of the city, where warring factions had brought turmoil and murder. He planned to have the two leaders of the rival parties with him on stage and join hands to show the people of Jamaica their commitment to bringing peace to the streets by decreasing political rivalry.

Just after the concert was announced, however, the government called an election for December 20. The political campaign brought renewed ghetto violence. Some protestors were angry with Bob's message of peace. On the eve of the concert, gunmen broke into his house and shot him.

In the confusion, the would-be assassins only wounded Bob, and he managed to escape into the hills outside Kingston. For a day, he tried to make up his mind about whether to hold the concert anyway. Finally, on December 5, he came on stage at the park in Kingston and played a brief set in defiance of the gunmen.

This was Bob's last appearance in Jamaica for nearly eighteen months. Immediately after the show, he left the country. During early 1977, he lived in London and began work on his next album, *Exodus*.

Making the Charts

In 1975, *Natty Dread* had been the Wailers' first album to make the U.S. charts at #92, and *Rastaman Vibration* had followed it, but *Exodus* was the album that truly established the band's status as international stars. The album remained on the U.K. charts for fifty-six weeks in a row, and its three singles—"Exodus," "Waiting in Vain," and "Jammin'"—were all hit songs.

In 1977, the band also played a week of concerts at London's Rainbow Theatre. This was their last London appearance for the decade.

The next year, the band followed up their chart success with *Kaya*, which hit #4 in the United Kingdom the first week after its release, though it did not do as well in the United States. *Kaya* was less political than most of Bob's other albums; it was a collection of love songs and **homages** to the power of *ganja*—marijuana, that is, the "wisdom weed." The album also offered two chart singles, "Satisfy My Soul" and "Is This Love." According to the Web site Rasta-Man-Vibration.com, Bob's love songs were significant because

> **"Marley would set the mood right but in that same breath there is a calling lovers to respect and honor each other. Love was to Marley more than just sexual ecstasy, it was a process of love and devotion."**

The band toured Europe and America throughout 1978. The series of shows provided a second live album, *Babylon by Bus*. The Wailers also broke new ground for reggae by playing in Australia, Japan, and New Zealand.

A Voice for Peace

The year 1978 was a significant one for Bob Marley. In April, he returned to Jamaica to play the One Love Peace Concert in front of Jamaica's prime minister, Michael Manley, as well as the leader of the opposition party, Edward Seaga. Bob hoped these political leaders would listen to what his music had to say about equality and justice

ROLLING STONE

Bob Marley
Rastaman with a Bullet
By Ed McCormack

THE BEACH BOYS TEST THE WATER
BY JIM MILLER

JAMAICA AT WAR
Stalking
the Beast
of Babylon
By Michael Thomas

PAT MOYNIHAN
Ruling-Class Hero
By Timothy Crouse

JIMMY PAGE
Beats the Devil
By Cameron Crowe

If you're a musician, you know you've hit it big when you're on the cover of the *Rolling Stone* magazine. And Bob's appearance on the cover of the August 1976 issue of the magazine was certainly an indication of his importance to the music scene. But not everything would turn out so good in 1976.

for all people. Next, Bob was invited to the United Nations in New York to receive the Medal of Peace. And at the end of the year, Bob visited Africa for the first time, going first to Kenya and then on to Ethiopia, the Rastafarians' spiritual home.

Survival, the Wailers' ninth album for Island Records, was released in the summer of 1979. The album cover showed all the flags of Africa's independent nations, symbolizing the Wailers' support for African **solidarity**. Included on the album was "Zimbabwe," a stirring anthem for the soon-to-be-liberated nation of Rhodesia, as well as "So Much Trouble in the World," "Ambush in the Night," and "Africa Unite." The album was followed by a forty-seven-concert tour that kicked off at Harlem's Apollo Theater.

At the start of the following year—a new decade—the Wailers flew to Gabon, where they were to make their African debut. Bob said of Africa:

> **Too many people going on like England and America are in the world. But there is a better life in Africa. I feel for Africa, I want to go there and write some music. Instead of New York, why can't we go to Ghana? Go to Nigeria—meet some people, learn a new language. You see, people are only seeking material vanity. Black people are so stubborn. They stay here because white people give them a big hotel and a floor to vacuum.**

For Bob, Africa was more than a dream; it was a reality that symbolized the place where black people could live in dignity and prosperity. In an interview with Rita Marley, she said that what motivated herself and Bob was

> **the unity of Africa, 'cause that's our theme: Africa Unite. We believe in the words of Marcus Garvey: 'Black man, when you get your king, you get God.' So we'll bring that unification, because we believe in God. It's not only for Ethiopia, it's a global thing. But we chose Ethiopia for the love of Ethiopia and for what Ethiopia stands for.**

Bob Marley was always about peace and justice. A bullet fired by a potential assassin couldn't stop him and his message. Neither could riots and other acts of violence. In 1978, he performed in a concert before Jamaican leaders, hoping to end long-lived conflict on the island. His efforts earned him a medal from the United Nations.

Bob was upset to discover, however, that the band would be playing for the country's young **elite**, members of the very group that the Wailers' music cried out against. The band was happier about their return trip to Africa a few months later, this time at the official invitation of the government of liberated Zimbabwe to play at the country's independence ceremony in April. Bob considered this to be the greatest honor his band had ever received. It demonstrated how important the Wailers were to the Third World.

While the band was in Zimbabwe, one of the leaders of the freedom movement invited Bob to make his home there. Bob told later how much the invitation meant to him:

> **"That was the best invitation you could get. Man who fight for the land tell you to stay. It's your home. Plenty people shoot after him and him still alive, come tell me to stay in Zimbabwe. It's the best."**

The Hits Continue

The band released its next album, *Uprising*, in May 1980. It was an instant hit, and the single "Could You Be Loved" became a massive worldwide seller. The album also featured "Coming in From the Cold," "Work," and "Redemption Song." This last song was based on the teaching of Marcus Garvey: "Emancipate yourself from mental slavery, none but ourselves can free our minds."

All these songs were more than just hits. Each was another affirmation of Bob's powerful and positive beliefs. He said:

> **"Life is one big road with lots of signs. So when you riding through the ruts, don't complicate your mind. Flee from hate, mischief and jealousy. Don't bury your thoughts; put your vision to reality. Wake Up and Live!"**

The Wailers embarked on a major European tour; their concerts broke records across the continent. The tour's schedule included a 100,000-capacity crowd in Milan, the biggest show in the band's history. Many music critics considered Bob Marley and the Wailers to be the most important band on the road that year, and their new *Uprising* album hit every chart in Europe.

Bob and the Wailers were full of optimism and excitement. They made plans for an American tour with Stevie Wonder, and the future looked bright. No one realized that tragedy was about to strike.

Some artists might have worried that singing about justice, equality, and prejudice might negatively influence record sales. Bob didn't care. He had principles, and record sales weren't going to get him to change. And his fans all over the world respected him for sticking to his beliefs; they bought his music and attended his concerts in droves.

Bob Marley was true to his religious beliefs, and it may have cost the music legend his life. When doctors wanted to amputate a cancerous toe, Bob refused because it went against his religion. The cancer spread and eventually caused his death. Did Bob make the wrong decision? Not for Bob, who remained true to his beliefs to the end.

Cancer

Bob Marley and the Wailers played two shows at New York City's Madison Square Garden, but immediately afterward, Bob became seriously ill. Three years earlier, in London, he had hurt a toe while playing football. When the wound was finally treated, doctors told him it was cancerous and recommended that he have his toe amputated. Bob was not willing to do this, though, as it was against his religious beliefs.

By 1980, the cancer had spread throughout Bob's body. He played a final concert in Pittsburgh, Pennsylvania, and then he concentrated on fighting the disease. His battle continued for eight months in Bavaria, where he was treated at Dr. Joseph Issels' clinic. Issels' nontoxic treatment was controversial, but for a time, Bob's condition seemed to stabilize. In April of 1981, Jamaica awarded him the Order of Merit, one of the nation's highest honors, in recognition of his outstanding contribution to the country's culture.

Eventually, however, the cancer spread to Bob's brain, and his body gave up the battle. At the beginning of May 1981, Bob left Europe to go home to Jamaica. He did not complete the journey, though. Instead, he died in a Miami hospital on Monday, May 11. Bob was thirty-six years old.

On Thursday, May 21, 1981, the people of Jamaica gave Robert Nesta Marley an official funeral. Following the service, attended by both the prime minister and the leader of the opposition, Marley's body was taken to his birthplace in the north of the island. It rests there in a mausoleum.

An Eternal Soul

Although Bob's earthly life and musical career had come to a too-early end, Bob believed firmly in the reality of eternal life. He said once:

> **"Life and Jah are one in the same. Jah is the gift of existence. I am in some way eternal, I will never be duplicated. The singularity of every man and woman is Jah's gift. What we struggle to make of it is our sole gift to Jah. The process of what that struggle becomes, in time, the Truth."**

Bob's life was a gift to both his God and to the world, a gift of truth. And his musical legacy has survived the years.

Though Bob Marley died in 1985, the influence of Bob Marley and the Wailers has lived on to this day. His wife and his children carry on his message, and his work, all over the world. Directing programs in Africa, Rita hopes to educate the poor through the efforts of a foundation that bear Bob's name.

5

Bob Marley's Legacy

"Money can't buy life." These words of advice for his son Ziggy were the last words Bob Marley spoke before he died. There was time when people wondered if Bob's children really understood their father's message—but as the years have passed, the world has seen Bob's family carry on his legacy as they take up his fight for justice.

Rita Marley

One of Bob's most powerful lines was "Get up, stand up, don't give up the fight"—and it's a line that still calls many to action, especially Bob's widow, Rita Marley. Today, she heads both the Bob Marley Foundation and the Rita Marley Foundation, organizations that work to end poverty in Jamaica and Africa. In July 2006, she told ABC's *Good Morning America*,

> **We have been funding ourselves in whatever we have been doing, especially in Ghana and Ethiopia. We've been doing it out of our own pockets in terms of what Bob left us. . . . [The greatest needs are] water, food, clothing, toothbrush to brush their teeth and someone to love them. So we have decided to give back to what is really in need and—and it's about not just black people, but every kind of people, you know.**

Rita Marley is part of a long list of celebrities who have taken up the fight for Africa. Brad Pitt, Angelina Jolie, Bono, Bill and Melinda Gates, and George Clooney are also drawing worldwide attention to this continent, ravaged by war and disease, where the average life expectancy is only forty-six. For Rita, it's an old fight, but she's glad for whatever help she can get. She told *Good Morning America*:

> **I like what Bono is doing, for instance, in Africa, by going down there and giving, giving and teaching. There are a few international people that's really putting help into Africa, and I'm so happy that I lived to see this, because I never dreamed that this would ever happen. But it's important that you can be an example to someone, somewhere, somehow.**

In 2006, Rita Marley worked with the Black-Eyed Peas in South Africa. They put on a concert in South Africa to benefit children there who are living with AIDS. Rita and the Black-Eyed Peas are also working to build schools there.

Rita stresses that you don't have to be an organization, have lots of money, or be a star to work to help Africa.

> **It doesn't have to be money. And I've taken clothing that my family has worn out. They think, 'Oh, well,**

I'm finished with that.' And when you go to Africa, it is like, 'Whooo, it's the first time I've ever had good shoes or had a good dress to wear.'**"**

Rita also sponsors thirty-five Ethiopian children, the youngest victims of war and AIDS. She, along with her family, have begun to organize concerts titled Africa Unite that take place on Bob's birthday, raising money and awareness in her husband's name.

Rita and Stephen Marley joined the Black Eyed Peas for the hip-hop group's performance at the Philadelphia venue of Live 8 on July 2, 2005. Rita and the Black Eyed Peas also joined forces the following year when the band performed a concert in South Africa to benefit children living with AIDS. They're also building schools in that country.

Rita told ABC she was confident her husband would see her work as "a dream come true."

> **"It's the reality, and it makes it easier for me to do because it's like the ground plan was made. It's done. This is what we would do if we could and now we can. So I think we're—we're getting his blessing. Because each time I look on his smiling face, [I] can see. He's saying, 'Good work, Rita.' Because yes, it's for real. This is what we wanted to do."**

Bob's Children

Bob and Rita Marley had thirteen children, including two they adopted. At least five of these children—Ziggy, Damian, Julian, Ky-mani, and Stephen—have become musicians in their own right. As the twentieth century drew to an end, however, some of Bob Marley's old friends criticized his children for not being more like their father. In Family Man's 1999 interview with Duggy Bones, he said:

> **"They are not following their father's footsteps: roots, culture and reality. They are trying to do other things like hip-hop and they don't even know what direction they are going in. They don't have no culture, they look like roots Rasta but they are in no way praising Jah or the orthodox. They are disguised in Church, some of them fancy clothes and cars and making some big offers in the Church but that's not it. . . . They running from reality."**

But by 2007, Bob's children seemed to have found a greater understanding of the meaning of their father's life. In an interview with BobMarley.com, Stephen Marley talked about his father's belief in the concept of "irie"—being totally at peace with your life, with absolutely no worries. No matter what political upheaval rocked his island home, Stephen remembers that his father always found a way to smile whenever he thought of Jamaica.

Music was obviously in Bob's genes, and he passed it along to some of his children. His youngest son, Damian, has become a big star in his own right. In 2002, he received a Grammy Award for Best Reggae Album. He won two more Grammys in 2006: Best Reggae Album and Best Urban/Alternative Performance.

Ziggy Marley has also earned a reputation as a musical artist. But Ziggy and the other Marley children inherited something else from Bob and Rita—the need to give back. Stephen and Ziggy formed Ghetto Youths' International, an organization that helps young, underprivileged artists get their start in the rough world of the music business.

Stephen Marley's debut solo CD, *Mind Control*, was released in March 2006. That same year, he and his brothers gave Jamaica a reason to smile by putting on a concert there for their father's sixty-second birthday celebration. The concert's proceeds benefited

Ghetto Youths' International, the foundation started by Stephen and his brother Ziggy to help young, underprivileged artists get a start in the music business. In memory of their father's famous December 5, 1976, concert—the memorable day when Bob performed in front of 80,000 fans in a Kingston park despite being shot two days earlier in an assassination attempt—his sons called their performance Smile Jamaica.

Stephen remembered that his father was constantly

> **"bringing positivity through music, not because of the situation in the world. And it's not good to talk about if you just talk about what's going on sometimes, you know? Positive things have to be the highlight. As him say, sometimes it takes one to say, 'Smile, man.' Once there's life, there's hope."**

A National Hero?

Bob Marley has been nominated to be named a National Hero of Jamaica. So far, however, the government of Jamaica has failed to move on the issue. The island already has seven official national heroes, the government points out: Marcus Garvey, the Pan-African leader and visionary; Paul Bogle and Sam Sharpe, rebel leaders; Alexander Bustamante and Norman Manley, prime ministers; George William Gordon, a politician and **orator**; and Nanny of the Maroons, a female revolutionary.

Those who advocate for Bob being officially named a national hero remember that Bob's life story was connected with all these Jamaican heroes. He adopted the philosophy of Marcus Garvey, a revered figure to many of the Rastafari faith; he wrote a lyric about Paul Bogle in the song "So Much Things to Say"; he brought together Bustamante and Manley during a unity concert; and through his work, he carried on the spirit of justice found in Gordon's work and the spirit of revolution in Nanny's successful campaign against the British.

Christopher John Farley, author of *Before the Legend: The Rise of Bob Marley*, favors the move to make Bob an official hero. He told BobMarley.com:

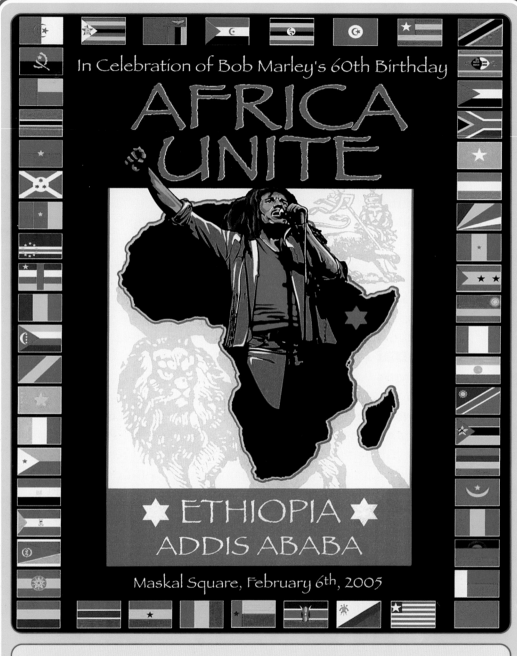

In Celebration of Bob Marley's 60th Birthday

AFRICA UNITE

★ ETHIOPIA ★
ADDIS ABABA

Maskal Square, February 6th, 2005

In Africa, especially in the country of Ethiopia, there are few heroes more revered than Bob Marley. Fans still listen to the music of Bob Marley and the Wailers, and remember the love and respect Bob had for the continent and country. In 2005, Bob's birthday celebration—his sixtieth—was held in Ethiopia.

"That's why Marley is such a perfect hero. He and his bandmates in the Wailers came from almost nothing and made it big. They made their own instruments, out of things like cans and string and wire. They created arguably the best debut recording ever with a budget that would barely pay for catering for other top musical acts of the time. They made it out of Nine Miles and Trench Town and Jamaica and became superstars in London and New York and Tokyo and Cape Town.**"**

The Legend Lives On

Whether or not Bob is ever named a national hero in his homeland, he is still a hero for many, a legend that never dies. In Africa, for example, especially Ethiopia, Bob Marley and the Wailers are still popular, and in 2005, Bob's sixtieth birthday celebration was held in Shashamane, Ethiopia. People in Jamaica want Bob's face to appear on their nation's 1,000-dollar note. In 2006, a Brooklyn community board voted to rename a part of Church Avenue after Bob Marley, pending approval of the New York City Council; the area runs through a heavily Caribbean American populated neighborhoods.

Bob has also received his share of more official recognitions. *Time* magazine named Bob Marley and the Wailers' *Exodus* as album of the twentieth century—and the BBC named their song "One Love" the song of the century. In 2001, a feature-length documentary about Marley's life by Jeremy Marre of Rebel Music was nominated for Best Long Form Music Video Documentary at the Grammys.

Most important, though, Bob's voice still challenges us all. "Open your eyes," Bob said more than once. "Look within. Are you satisfied with the life you're living?"

1930 Ras Tafari Makonnen is crowned emperor of Ethiopia.

1945 Robert Nesta Marley is born.

1962 Bob auditions for Leslie Kong.

1963 Bob Marley and the Wailing Wailers audition for Clement Dodd, who agrees to record them.

"Simmer Down," the group's first single, is released.

1964 **January** "Simmer Down" hits #1 on the Jamaican music charts.

1966 **February 10** Bob and Rita Anderson are married.

1967 Bob and the Wailers' record label, Wail 'N' Soul, folds.

1970 Aston "Family Man" Barrett and Carlton Barrett join the Wailers.

1971 Bob accompanies Johnny Nash to Sweden.

Bob and the Wailers sign with Blackwell.

1973 **April** Bob and the Wailers begin a club tour.

Burnin' is released.

1975 Bunny and Peter quit the band and are replaced by the I-Threes.

Natty Dread becomes the group's first album to make the U.S. charts.

1976 *Rastaman Vibration* is released and cracks the U.S. charts at #8.

December 3 A gunman breaks into Bob's home and shoots him.

December 5 Bob performs a free concert in Kingston.

1977 The band plays a week of concerts at the Rainbow Theatre in London.

1978 The band tours Europe and the United States.

Bob receives the Medal of Peace from the United Nations.

Bob goes to Africa for the first time.

April Bob plays the One Love Peace Concert in Jamaica.

1980 Cancer is found to have spread throughout Bob's body.

Bob plays his last concert.

1981 **April** Jamaica awards Bob the Order of Merit for his outstanding contribution to Jamaican culture.

May 11 Bob Marley dies from cancer.

May 21 Bob receives a state funeral in Jamaica.

1991 Music from a live concert held at KSAN almost twenty years before is released as *Talkin' Blues*.

1994 Bob Marley is inducted into the Rock and Roll Hall of Fame.

2001 A feature-length documentary about Marley's life by Jeremy Marre of Rebel Music is nominated for Best Long Form Music Video Documentary at the Grammys.

February 6 Bob gets a star on the Hollywood Walk of Fame in honor of his fifty-sixth birthday.

2005 Bob's sixtieth birthday celebration is held in Shashamane, Ethiopia.

2006 Rita Marley works in South Africa with the Black-Eyed Peas to benefit children living with AIDS and to build schools.

March Stephen Marley releases his debut CD.

March The Marley brothers stage a Smile Concert for Bob's sixty-second birthday.

A Brooklyn community board votes to rename a part of Church Avenue after Bob Marley, pending approval of the New York City Council.

Select Albums

1966   *The Wailing Wailers*

1970   *The Best of the Wailers*
         Soul Rebels

1971   *Soul Revolution*
         Soul Revolution Part II

1973   *African Herbsman*
         Catch a Fire
         Burnin'

1974   *Rasta Revolution*
         Natty Dread

1975   *Live!*

1976   *Rastaman Vibration*

1977   *Exodus*

1978   *Kaya*
         Babylon by Bus

1979   *Survival*

1980   *Uprising*

1981   *Interviews*

1983   *Confrontation*

1984   *Legend*

1986   *Rebel Music*

1991   *Talkin' Blues*

1992   *Songs of Freedom*

1995   *Natural Mystic: The Legend Lives On*

1999   *Bob Marley: Reggae Legend*

2001   *One Love: The Very Best of Bob Marley & The Wailers*

2002   *Bob Marley and The Wailers: Trenchtown Rock*
         (Anthology '69–'78)

2003 *Live at the Roxy*

2005 *Gold*
Africa Unite: The Singles Collection

Videos

1984 *Bob Marley and the Wailers: Legend*

1992 *Bob Marley: Time Will Tell*

1997 *Marley Magic Live*

2001 *Rebel Music: The Bob Marley Story*

2003 *Bob Marley—Spiritual Journey*
Legend: The Best of Bob Marley and the Wailers
The Legend Live

2004 *Bob Marley and the Wailers Live at the Rainbow*
2006 *Bits and Pieces About Bob Marley*
Catch a Fire

2007 *Music in Review: Bob Marley*

Awards and Recognitions

1976 *Rolling Stone* names Bob Marley and the Wailers Band of the Year.

1978 Receives the Peace Medal of the Third World from the United Nations.

1981 Receives the Jamaican Order of Merit.

1994 Inducted into the Rock and Roll Hall of Fame.

1999 *Time* magazine names *Exodus* Album of the Century.

2001 Receives a star on the Hollywood Walk of Fame; awarded Grammy Lifetime Achievement Award; a BBC poll ranks Bob as one of the greatest lyricists of all time.

2004 *Rolling Stone* ranks Bob #11 on their list of the 100 Greatest Artists of All Time.

Books

Borobwitz, Hank (ed.). *Every Little Thing Gonna Be Alright: The Bob Marley Reader.* New York: Perseus, 2004.

Bradley, Lloyd. *This Is Reggae Music: The Story of Jamaica's Music.* New York: Grove/Atlantic, 2001.

Farley, Christopher John. *Before the Legend: The Rise of Bob Marley.* New York: HarperCollins, 2006

Goldman, Vivien. *Book of Exodus: The Making and Meaning of Bob Marley and the Wailers' Album of the Century.* New York: Random House, 2006.

Henke, James. *Marley Legend: An Illustrated Life of Bob Marley.* San Francisco, Calif.: Chronicle Books, 2006.

Marley, Rita, and Hettie Jones. *No Woman No Cry: My Life With Bob Marley.* New York: Hyperion, 2005.

Sheridan, Maureen. *Bob Marley: Soul Rebel.* New York: Thunder Mouth's Press, 1999.

White, Timothy. *Catch a Fire: The Life of Bob Marley.* New York: Henry Holt, 2006.

Web Sites

home.c2i.net/cyberia/reggae/bob/bob_marley.html
Bob Marley & the Wailers

www.bobmarley.com
Bob Marley Home: The Official Site

www.bobmarleymovement.com
Bob Marley Movement of Jah People

www.pbs.org/wnet/americanmasters/database/Marley_b.html
American Masters: Bob Marley

advocated—Supported or spoke in favor of something.

aspiring—Seeking to attain a particular goal.

commemorative—Something that honors the memory of a person or event.

dub—A type of poetry in which words are spoken over reggae rhythms.

elite—A small group of individuals within a larger group who have more power, social standing, wealth, or talent than the rest of the group.

entrepreneur—Someone who assumes the risks and benefits of running a business.

genre—One of the categories that artistic works of all kinds can be divided into on the basis of form, style, or subject matter.

homages—Expressions of reverence and respect toward someone.

inducted—To formally install someone in an organization.

mentor—A more experienced person who provides guidance to someone with less experience.

optimism—The tendency to expect the best from a person or situation.

orator—Someone who gives speeches.

posthumous—Occurring after death.

procured—Acquired.

quartermaster—A military officer who is responsible for providing soldiers with food, clothing, equipment, and living quarters.

solidarity—Harmony of interests and responsibilities among individuals in a group.

tenet—Any of a set of established and fundamental beliefs.

Rosa Waters has a degree in creative writing, and has written articles for various publications, as well as several titles in the Mason Crest Hip-Hop series. She has worked in an inner-city crisis center, and she knows firsthand some of the injustices blacks still face. Although she makes no claim to musical talent of her own, her husband is active in the music scene, and the interface between creativity, spirituality, and culture is one of her ongoing interests.

Picture Credits

page